the complete g

swimming
front crawl

learn, improve and fine-tune basic front crawl technique

fully illustrated with practical exercises

mark young

2nd Edition

A Catalogue record for this book is available from the British Library

ISBN 978-0-9570031-1-8

First published 2010 by Educate & Learn Publishing, Hertfordshire, UK
enquiries@educateandlearnpublishing.com

Graphics by Mark Young, courtesy of Poser V6.0

Design and typeset by Mark Young and Baines Design, Cuffley, UK

Published in association with swim-teach.com
www.swim-teach.com

Contents

front crawl

body position, legs, arms, breathing and timing

Front crawl is the fastest, most efficient stroke of them all. This is largely down to the streamlined body position and continuous propulsion from the arms and legs.

The alternating action of the arms and legs is relatively easy on the joints and the stroke as a whole develops aerobic capacity faster than any other stroke. In competitive terms it is usually referred to as Freestyle.

The constant alternating arm action generates almost all of the propulsion and is the most efficient arm action of all strokes. The leg action promotes a horizontal, streamlined body position and balances the arm action but provides little propulsion.

Freestyle breathing technique requires the head to be turned so that the mouth clears the water but causes minimal upset to the balance of the body from its normal streamlined position.

The timing and coordination of front crawl arms and legs occurs most commonly with six leg kicks to one arm cycle. However, stroke timing can vary, with a four beat cycle and even a one beat cycle, which is most commonly used in long distance swims and endurance events.

body position

The overall body position for this swimming stroke is streamlined and as flat as possible at the water surface with the head in-line with the body.

The waterline is around the natural hairline with eyes looking forward and down.

If the position of the head is raised it will cause the position of the hips and legs to lower which in turn will increase frontal resistance.

If the head position is too low it will cause the legs to raise and the kick to lose its efficiency.

Shoulders remain at the surface and roll with the arm action. Hips also roll with the stroke technique, close to the water surface and the legs remain in line with the body.

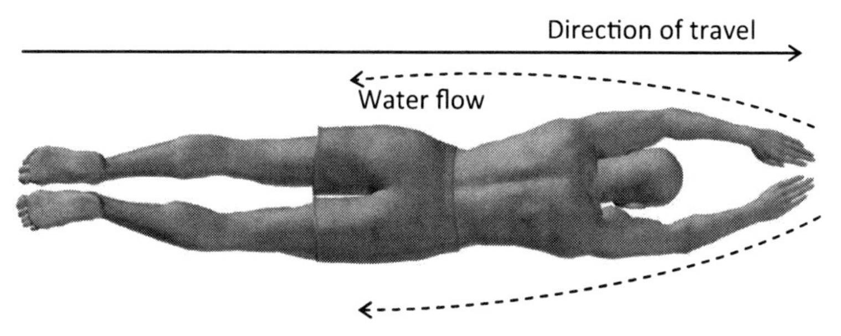

Streamlined body position minimises drag, allowing efficient movement through the water

legs

The leg kick for front crawl should originate from the hip and both legs should kick with equal force.

Legs kick in an up and down alternating action, with the propulsive phase coming from the down kick. There should be a slight bend in the knee caused by the water pressure, and helps to produce the propulsion required on the down kick.

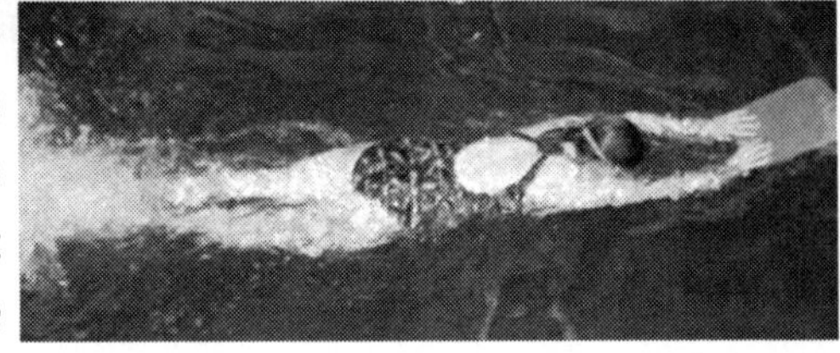

The downward kick begins at the hip and uses the thigh muscles to straighten the leg at the knee, ending with the foot extended to allow it's surface area to bear upon the water. As the leg moves upwards, the sole of the foot and the back of the leg press upwards and backwards against the water.

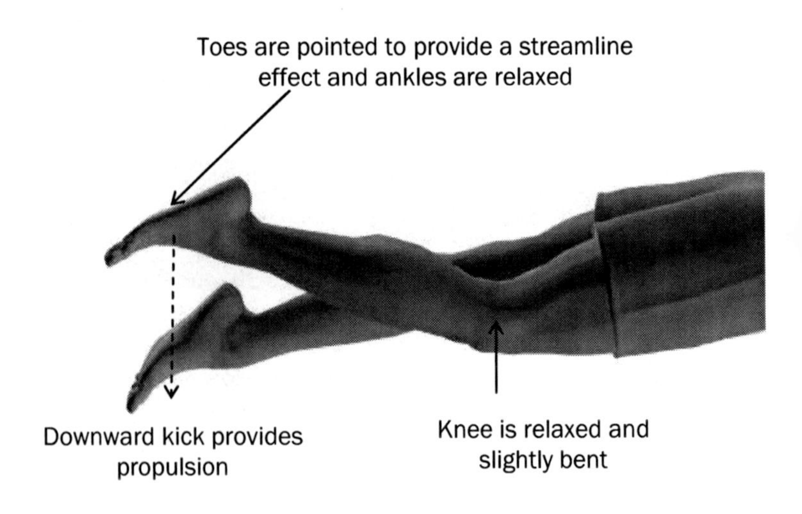
Toes are pointed to provide a streamline effect and ankles are relaxed
Downward kick provides propulsion
Knee is relaxed and slightly bent

The upward kick slows and stops as the leg nears and minimally breaks the water surface. Ankles are relaxed and toes pointed to give an in-toeing effect when kicking and leg kick depth should be within the overall depth of the body.

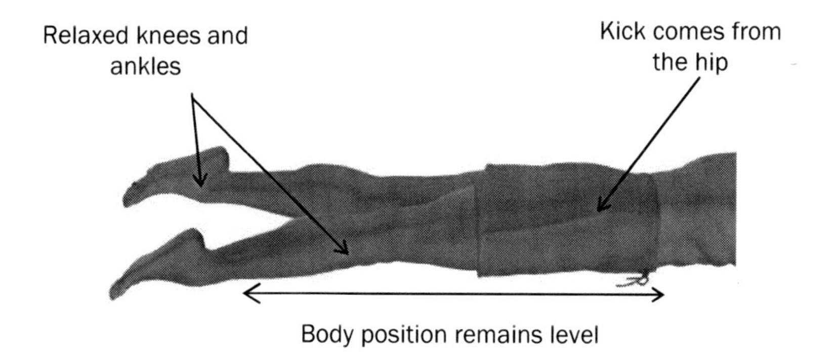
Relaxed knees and ankles
Kick comes from the hip
Body position remains level

arms

The continuous alternating arm action provides the majority of the power and propulsion of the entire swimming stroke.

- entry

The hand enters the water at a 45 degree angle, finger tips first, thumb side down. Hand entry should be between shoulder and head line with a slight elbow bend.

- catch

The hand reaches forward under the water without over stretching. Arm fully extends just under the water surface.

- propulsive Phase

Hand sweeps through the water downward, inwards and then upwards. Elbow is high at the end of the down sweep and remains high throughout the in-sweep. Hand pulls through towards the thigh and upwards to the water surface.

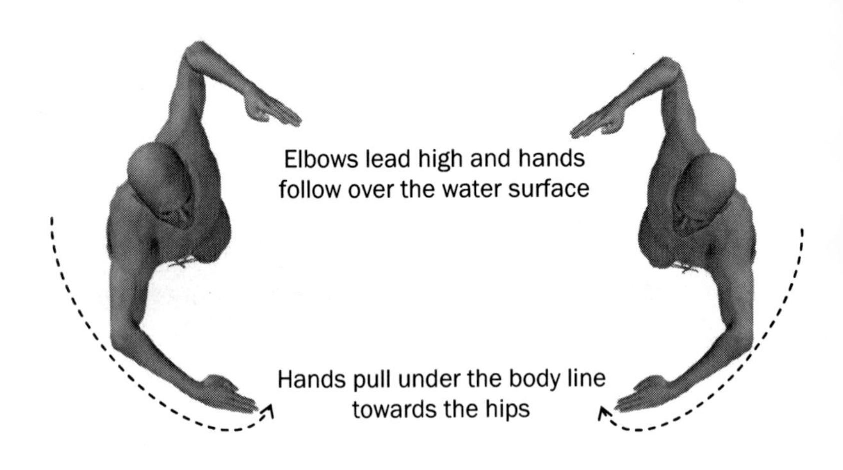
Elbows lead high and hands follow over the water surface
Hands pull under the body line towards the hips

- recovery phase

The elbow bends to exit the water first. Hand and fingers fully exit the water and follow a straight line along the body line over the water surface. Elbow is bent and high and the arm is fully relaxed.

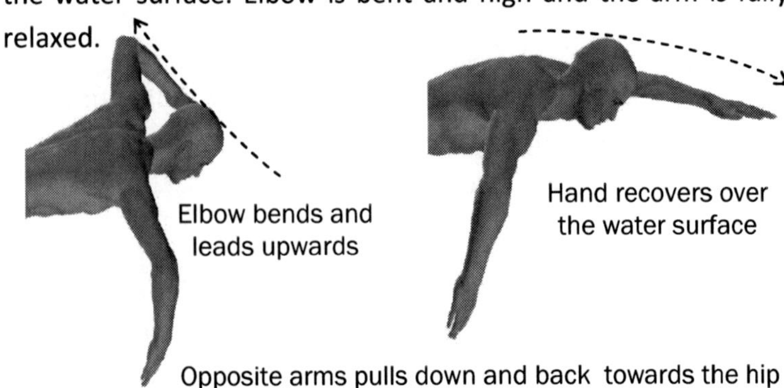
Elbow bends and leads upwards
Hand recovers over the water surface
Opposite arms pulls down and back towards the hip

breathing

The head turns to the side on inhalation for freestyle breathing technique. The head begins to turn at the end of the upward arm sweep and turns enough for the mouth to clear the water and inhale. The head turns back into the water just as the arm recovers over and the hand returns to the water. Breathing can be bilateral (alternating sides every one and a half stroke cycles) or unilateral (same side) depending of the stroke cycle and distance to be swum.

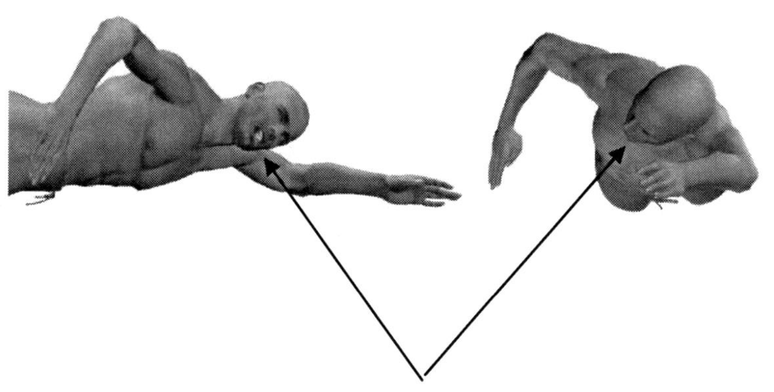

Breath IN as the arm pulls through and the head turns to the side

Types of Breathing

- Trickle

The breath is slowly exhaled through the mouth and nose into the water during the propulsive phase of the arm pull. The exhalation is controlled to allow inhalation to take place easily as the head turns and the arm recovers.

Types of Breathing continued.

- Explosive

The breath is held after inhalation during the propulsive arm phase and then released explosively, part in and part out of the water, as the head is turned to the side.

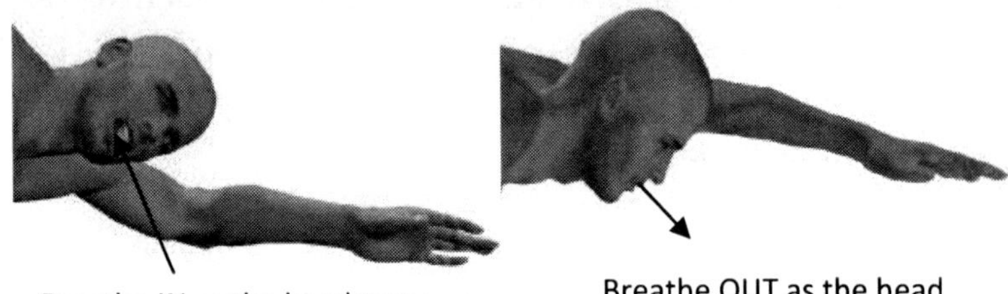

Breathe IN as the head turns out of the water

Breathe OUT as the head faces forward and down

timing

The timing and coordination for this swimming stroke usually occurs naturally.

Arms should provide a continuous power and propulsive alternating action whilst leg kicks also remain continuous and alternating.

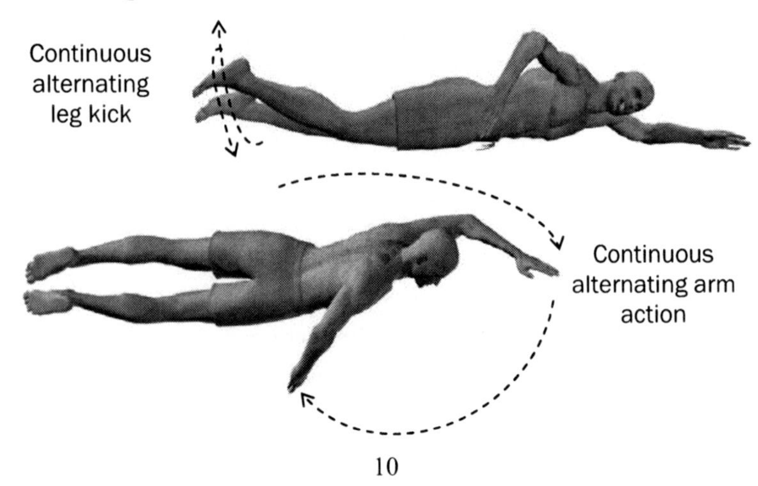

However, there are a few timing variations.

- Six beat cycle – each leg kicks three down kicks per arm cycle. The cycle is normally taught to beginners and used by sprint swimmers.
- Four beat cycle – each leg kicks down twice for each arm pull.
- One-beat cycle – each leg kicks one downbeat per arm pull. This timing cycle is normally used by long distance swimmers, where the leg kick acts as a counter balance instead of a source of propulsion.

full stroke overview

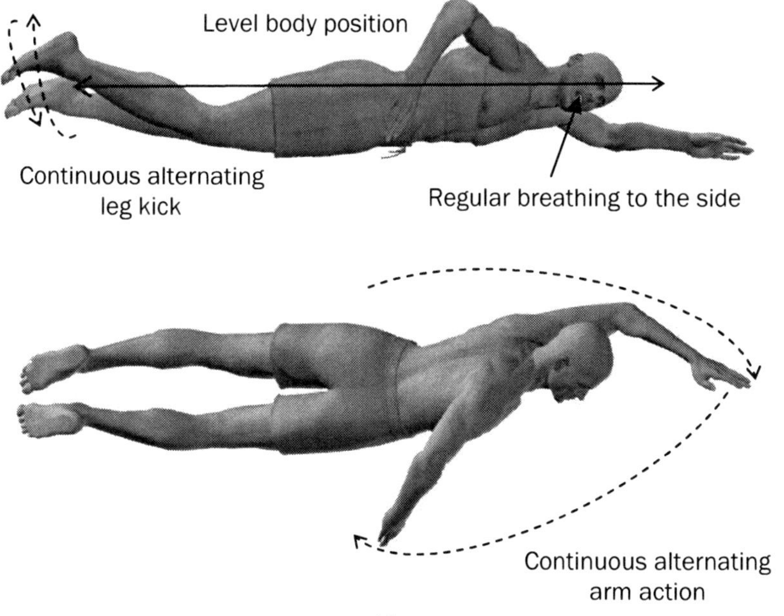

“The water is your friend...you don't have to fight with water, just share the same spirit as the water, and it will help you move”.

Alexandr Popov - Olympic Gold Medallist

front crawl

stroke exercises

The stroke exercises contained in the following part of this book form a reference section for each aspect of front crawl swimming stroke.

what are they?

Each specific exercise focuses on a certain aspect of the swimming stroke, for example the body position, the leg kick, the arms, the breathing or the timing and coordination, all separated into easy-to-learn stages. Each one contains a photograph of the exercise being performed, a graphical diagram and all the technique elements and key focus points that are relevant to that particular exercise.

how will they help?

They break down your swimming stroke into its core elements and then force you to focus on that certain area. For example if you are performing a leg kick exercise, the leg kick is isolated and therefore your focus and concentration is only on the legs. The technical information and key focus points then fix your concentration on the most important elements of the leg kick. The result: a more efficient and technically correct leg kick. The same then goes for exercises for the arms, breathing, timing and coordination and so on.

will they improve your swimming strokes?

Yes, definitely! These practical exercises not only isolate certain areas but can highlight your bad habits. Once you've worked though each element of the stroke and practiced the exercises a few times, you will slowly eliminate your bad habits. The result: a more efficient and technically correct swimming stroke, swum with less effort!

The page layouts for each exercise follow the same format, keeping all relevant information on an easy-to-follow double page. The aims, technical focuses and key points are all listed with a photograph and graphical diagram of the exercise along with the most common mistakes.

Body Position: Holding the poolside

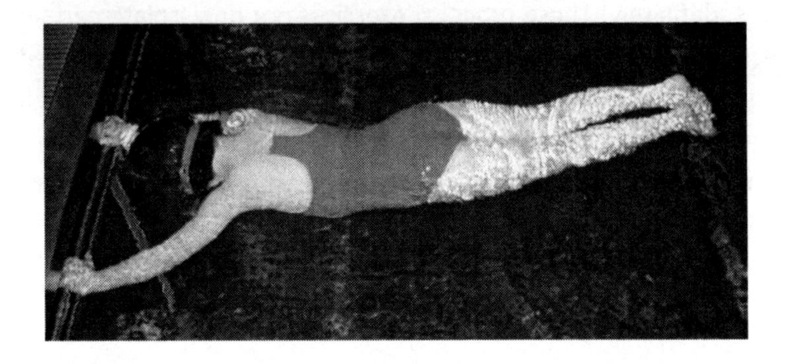

Aim: to encourage confidence in a floating position.

The swimmer holds the poolside for added security. Some assistance may be required as some people will not naturally float.

Technical Focus

- Head is central and still
- Face is submerged
- Eyes are looking downwards
- Shoulders should be level
- Hips are close to the surface
- Legs are together and in line with the body

Key Actions

- Relax
- Keep the head tucked between the arms
- Stretch out as far as you can
- Keep your feet together

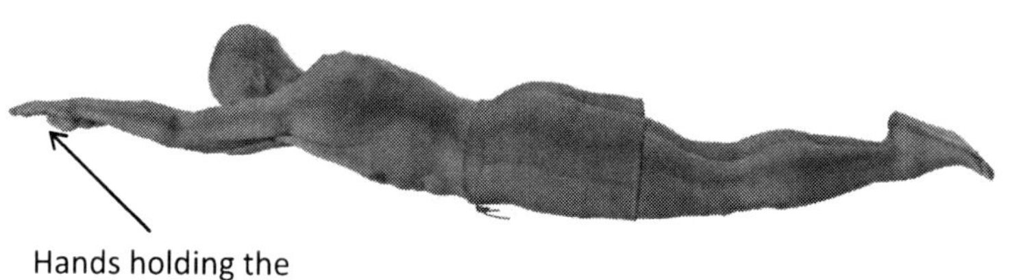

Overall body position is as horizontal as possible, depending on the swimmers own buoyancy.

Common Faults

- Failure to submerge the face
- Overall body is not relaxed
- Head is not central
- Whole body is not remaining straight
- Feet are not together

Body Position: Static practice holding floats

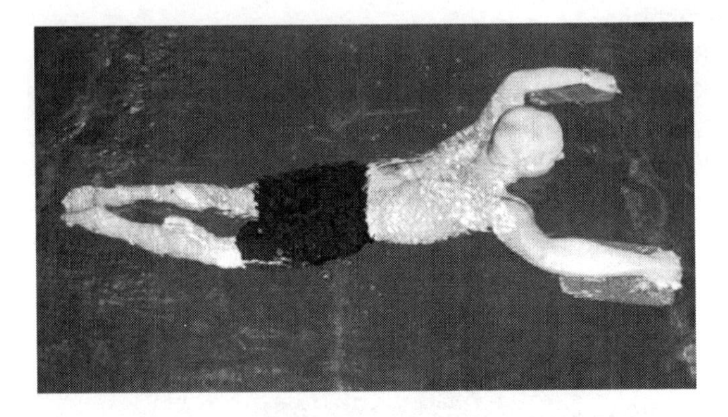

Aim: to help the swimmer develop confidence in their own buoyancy.

A float can be held under each arm or a single float held out in front, depending on levels of confidence and ability. Some swimmers may need extra assistance if they lack natural buoyancy.

Technical Focus

- Head is central and still
- Face is submerged
- Eyes are looking downwards
- Shoulders should be level
- Hips are close to the surface
- Legs are together and in line with the body

Key Actions

- o Relax
- o Keep the head tucked between the arms
- o Stretch out as far as you can
- o Keep your feet together

Overall body position is horizontal and as flat as possible
Float held in each hand or single float held in both hands

Common Faults

- o Failure to submerge the face
- o Head is not central
- o Whole body is not remaining straight
- o Feet and hands are not together

Body Position: Push and glide from standing

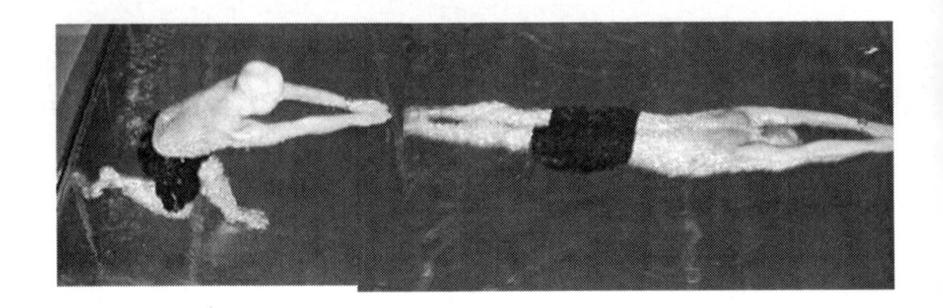

Aim: to develop correct body position and confidence in pushing off.

The swimmer starts with arms stretched out in front and pushes off from the pool floor or from the wall with one foot and glides through the water unaided.

Technical Focus

- Initial push should be enough to gain good movement
- Head remains still and central
- Face submerged so that the water is at brow level
- Shoulders should be level
- Legs in line with the body

Key Actions

- Push hard from the side/pool floor
- Keep your head tucked between your arms
- Stretch out as far as you can
- Keep your hands together
- Keep your feet together

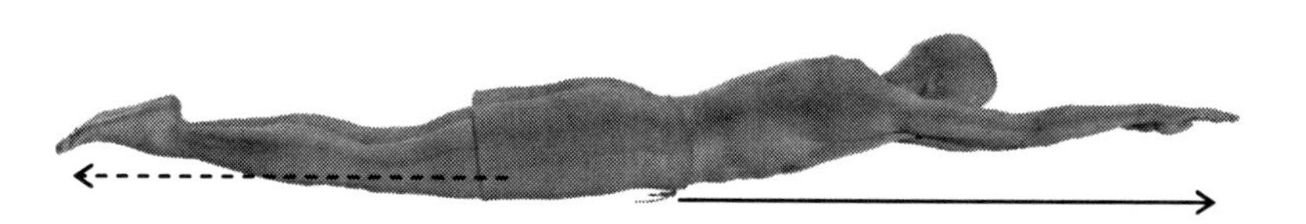
Legs push off from pool
side or pool floor
Direction of travel

Common Faults

- Failure to submerge the face
- Push off is too weak
- Whole body is not remaining straight
- Feet are not together

Body Position: Push and glide from the side holding floats

Aim: to develop correct body position whilst moving through the water.

Body position should be laying prone with the head up at this stage. The use of floats helps to build confidence, particularly in the weak or nervous swimmer. The floats create a slight resistance to the glide, but this is still a useful exercise.

Technical Focus

- Head remains still and central with the chin on the water surface
- Eyes are looking forwards and downwards
- Shoulders should be level and square
- Hips are close to the surface
- Legs are in line with the body

Key Actions

- o Push hard from the wall
- o Relax and float across the water
- o Keep your head still and look forward
- o Stretch out as far as you can
- o Keep your feet together

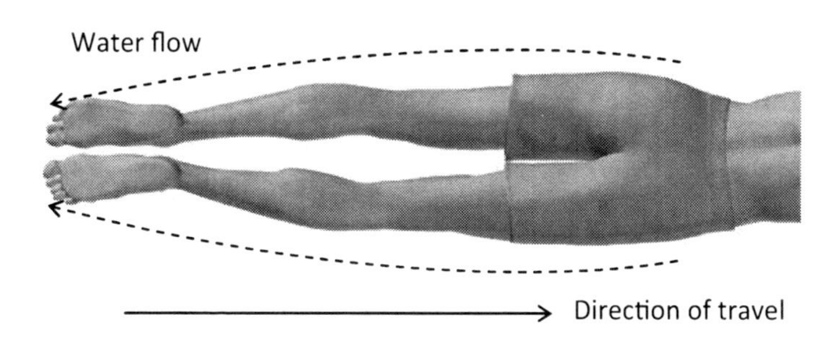

Common Faults

- o Push from the side is not hard enough
- o Head is not central
- o Whole body is not remaining straight
- o Feet are not together

Body Position: Push and glide off the poolside

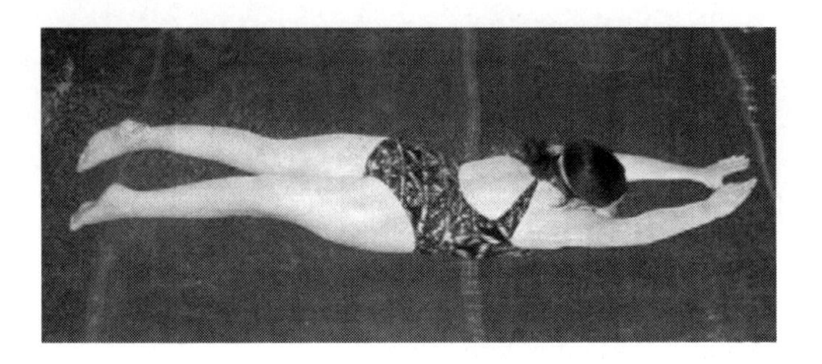

Aim: to develop a streamlined body position whilst moving thorough the water.

Movement is created by pushing and gliding from holding position at the poolside.

Technical Focus

- o Head remains still and central
- o Face submerged so that the water is at brow level
- o Shoulders should be level and square
- o Legs are in line with the body
- o Overall body position should be streamlined

Key Actions

- Push hard from the side
- Stretch your arms out in front as you push
- Keep your head tucked between your arms
- Stretch out as far as you can
- Keep your hands and feet together

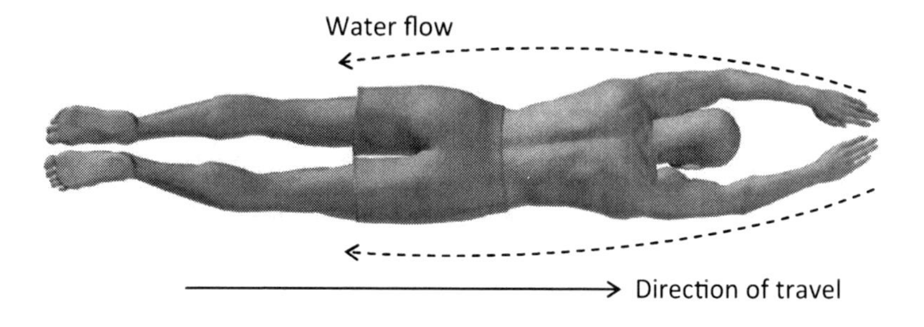

Streamlined body position minimises drag, allowing efficient movement through the water

Common Faults

- Push off is too weak
- Arms stretch in front after the push
- Head is not central
- Overall body position not in line
- Hands or feet are not together

Legs: Sitting on the poolside kicking

Aim: to give the swimmer the feel of the water during the kick.

Sitting on pool side kicking is an ideal exercise for the beginner to practise correct leg kicking action with the added confidence of sitting on the poolside.

Technical Focus

- Kick is continuous and alternating
- Knee is only slightly bent
- Legs are close together when they kick
- Ankles are relaxed and the toes are pointed.

Key Actions

- Kick with straight legs
- Pointed toes
- Make a small splash with your toes
- Kick with floppy feet
- Kick continuously

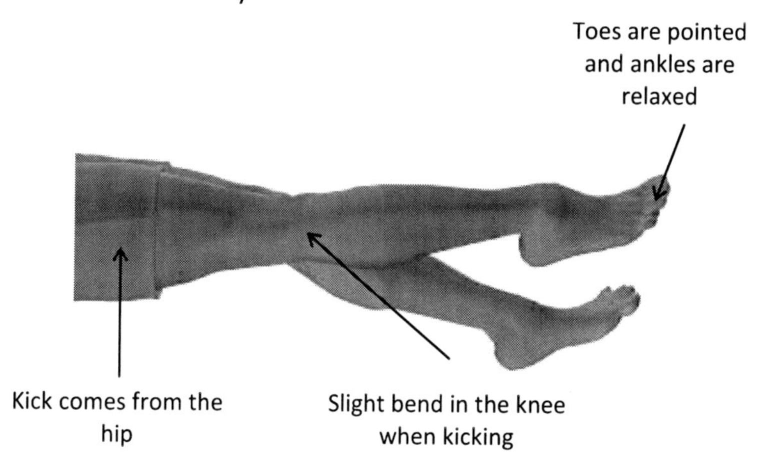
Toes are pointed and ankles are relaxed
Kick comes from the hip
Slight bend in the knee when kicking

Common Faults

- Knees bend too much
- Kick comes from the knee
- Stiff ankles

Legs: Holding the poolside

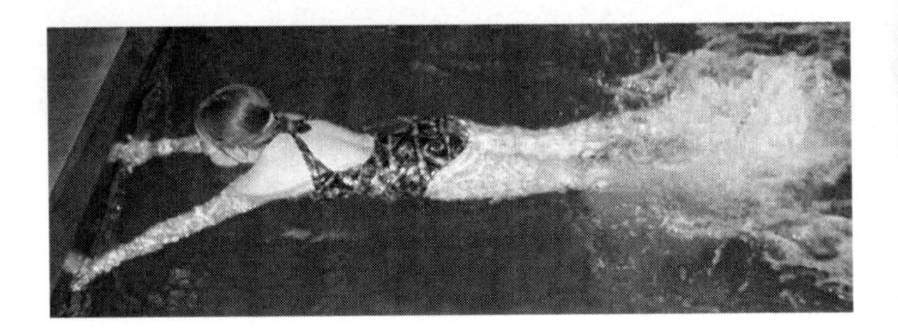

Aim: to encourage the swimmer to learn the kicking action.

Holding the poolside enhances confidence and helps develop leg strength and technique.

Technical Focus

- Kick comes from the hip
- Kick is continuous and alternating
- Knee is only slightly bent
- Legs are close together when they kick
- Ankles are relaxed and the toes are pointed
- Kick should just break the water surface

Key Actions

- o Kick with straight legs
- o Pointed toes
- o Make a small splash with your toes
- o Kick with floppy feet
- o Kick from your hips
- o Kick continuously
- o Legs kick close together

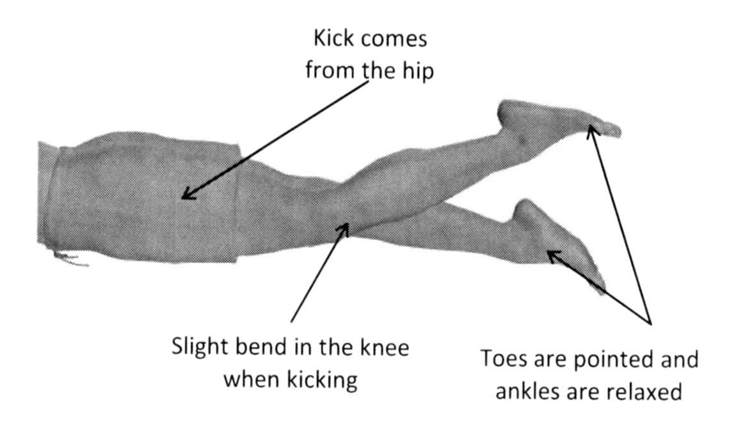
Kick comes from the hip
Slight bend in the knee when kicking
Toes are pointed and ankles are relaxed

Common Faults

- o Feet come out of the water
- o Kick comes from the knee
- o Legs are too deep in the water

Legs: Legs kick with a float held under each arm

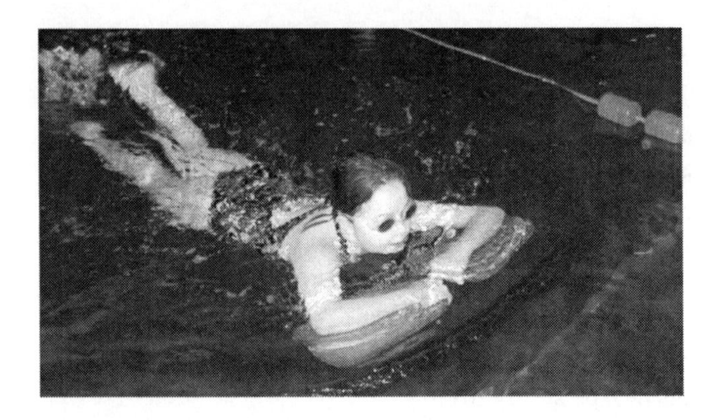

Aim: to learn correct kicking technique and develop leg strength.

The added stability of two floats will help boost confidence in the weak swimmer.

Technical Focus

- Kick comes from the hip
- Kick is continuous and alternating
- Chin remains on the water surface
- Legs are close together when they kick
- Ankles are relaxed and the toes are pointed
- Kick should just break the water surface
- Upper body and arms should be relaxed

Key Actions

- Kick with straight legs
- Pointed toes
- Kick with floppy feet
- Kick from your hips
- Kick continuously

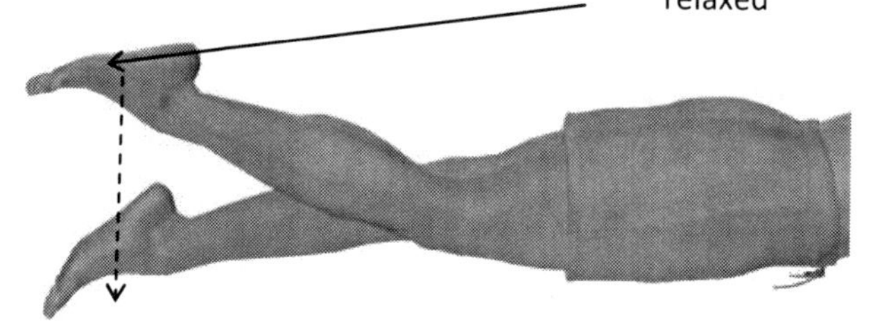
Toes are pointed to provide streamline effect and ankles are relaxed
Downward kick provides propulsion

Common Faults

- Head lifts above the surface, causing the legs to sink
- Kick comes from the knee causing excessive bend
- Kick is not deep enough
- Legs are too deep in the water

Legs: Float held with both hands

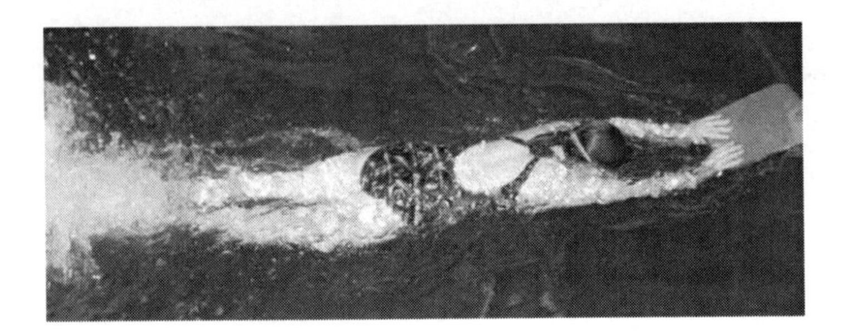

Aim: to practise and learn correct kicking technique.

Holding a float or kickboard out in front isolates the legs, encourages correct body position and develops leg strength.

Technical Focus

- Kick comes from the hip
- Kick is continuous and alternating.
- Legs are close together when they kick
- Ankles are relaxed and the toes are pointed.
- Kick should just break the water surface.

Key Actions

- Kick with pointed toes
- Make a small splash with your toes
- Kick with floppy feet
- Legs kick close together

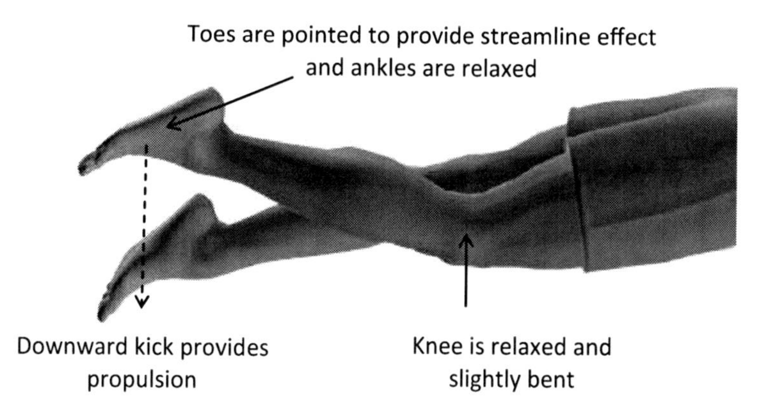
Toes are pointed to provide streamline effect and ankles are relaxed
Downward kick provides propulsion
Knee is relaxed and slightly bent

Common Faults

- Knees bend too much
- Feet come out of the water
- Kick comes from the knee
- Legs are too deep in the water

Legs: Push and glide with added leg kick

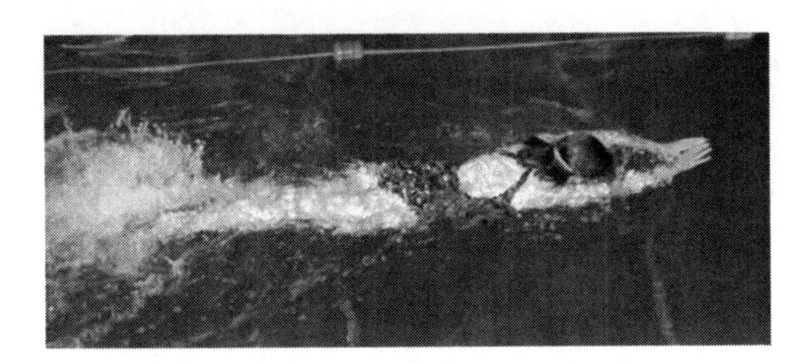

Aim: to develop correct body position and leg kick whilst holding the breath.

Push and glide without a float and add a leg kick whilst maintaining a streamlined body position.

Technical Focus

- Kick comes from the hip
- Streamlined body position is maintained
- Kick is continuous and alternating
- Legs are close together when they kick
- Ankles are relaxed and the toes are pointed
- Kick should just break the water surface

Key Actions

- Kick with straight legs and pointed toes
- Kick with floppy feet
- Kick from your hips
- Kick continuously

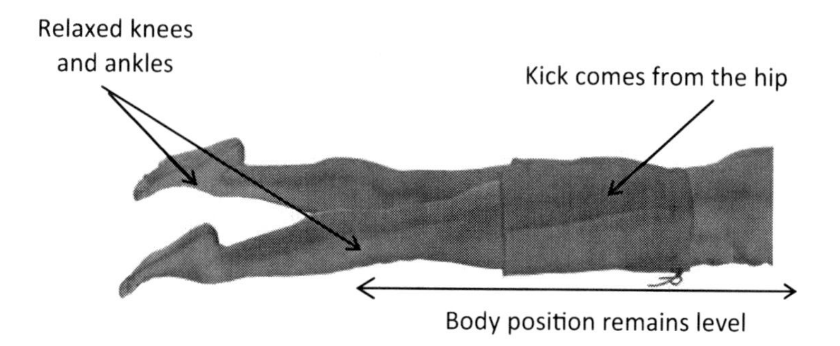
Relaxed knees
and ankles
Kick comes from the hip
Body position remains level

Common Faults

- Feet come out of the water
- Stiff ankles
- Kick is not deep enough
- Legs are too deep in the water

Legs: Leg kick holding a float vertically in front

Aim: to create resistance and help develop strength and stamina.

Holding a float vertically in front increases frontal resistance and therefore the intensity of the kicking action required. This helps to develops leg strength and stamina.

Technical Focus

- Kick comes from the hip
- Streamlined body position is maintained
- Kick is continuous and alternating
- Legs are close together when they kick
- Ankles are relaxed and the toes are pointed
- Kick should just break the water surface

Key Actions

- Kick with straight legs and pointed toes
- Kick with floppy feet
- Kick from your hips
- Kick continuously

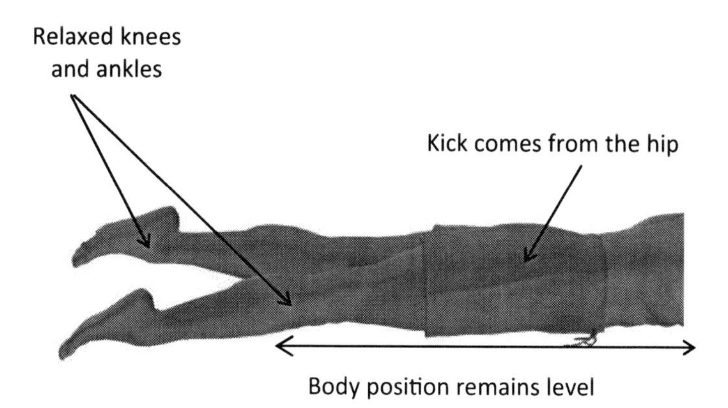
Relaxed knees and ankles
Kick comes from the hip
Body position remains level

Common Faults

- Feet come out of the water
- Stiff ankles
- Kick is not deep enough
- Legs are too deep in the water

Arms: Standing on the poolside or in shallow water

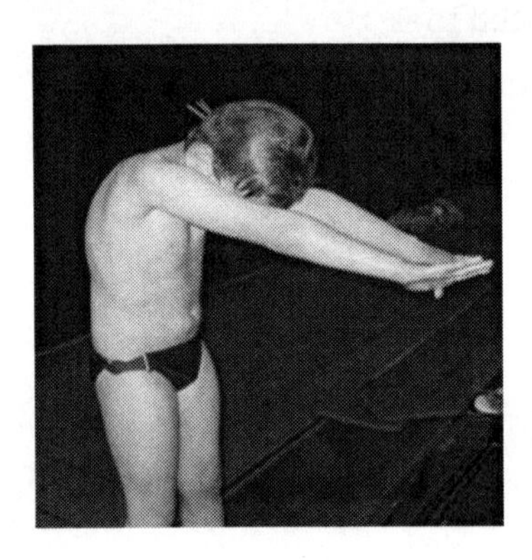

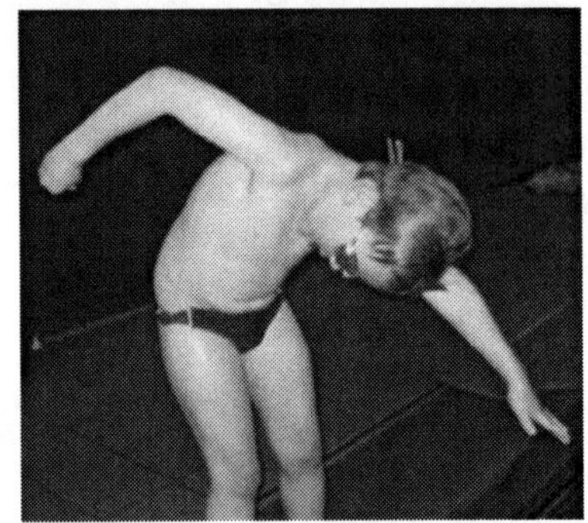

Aim: to practise correct arm movement whilst in a static position.

This is an exercise for beginners that can be practised on the poolside or standing in shallow water.

Technical Focus

- Fingers should be together
- Pull through to the hips
- Elbow bends and leads upwards

Key Actions

- Keep your fingers together
- Continuous smooth action
- Brush your hand past your thigh
- Gradually bend your elbow

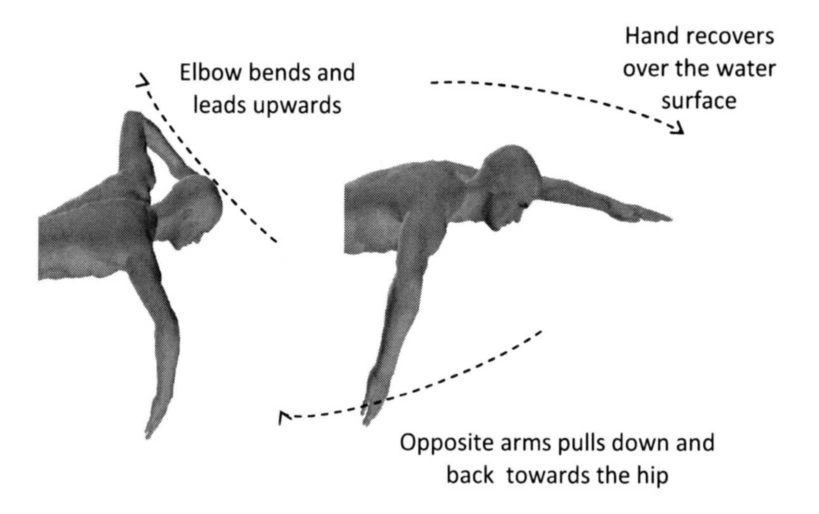
Elbow bends and
leads upwards
Hand recovers
over the water
surface
Opposite arms pulls down and
back towards the hip

Common Faults

- Fingers are too wide apart
- Pull is short and not to the thigh
- Arms are too straight as they pull
- Arms are too straight on recovery
- Hand entry is wide of the shoulder line

Arm: Single arm practice with float in one hand

Aim: to practise and improve correct arm technique

This practice allows the swimmer to develop arm technique whilst maintaining body position and leg kick. Holding a float with one hand gives the weaker swimmer security and allows the competent swimmer to focus on a single arm.

Technical Focus

- Fingertips enter first with thumb side down
- Fingers should be together
- Pull should be an elongated 'S' shape
- Pull through to the hips
- Elbow exits the water first
- Fingers clear the water on recovery

Key Actions

- Keep your fingers together
- Brush your hand past your thigh
- Pull fast under the water
- Make an 'S' shape under the water
- Elbow out first
- Reach over the water surface

Elbow leads out of the water first

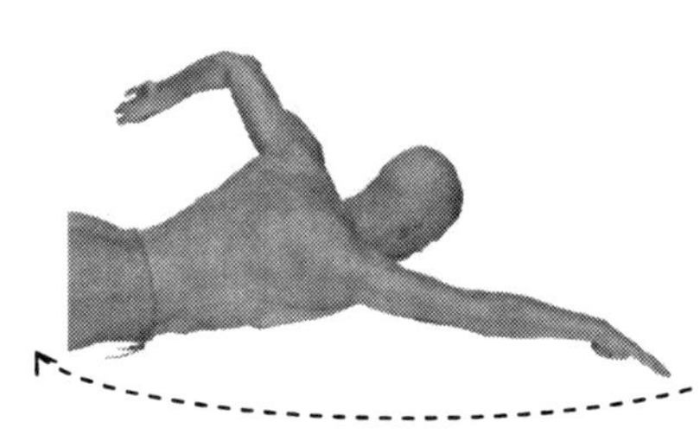

Arm pulls back through the water towards the hip

Common Faults

- Fingers are apart
- Pull is short and not to the thigh
- Lack of power in the pull
- Arm pull is too deep underwater
- Arms are too straight on recovery

Arms: Alternating arm pull whilst holding a float

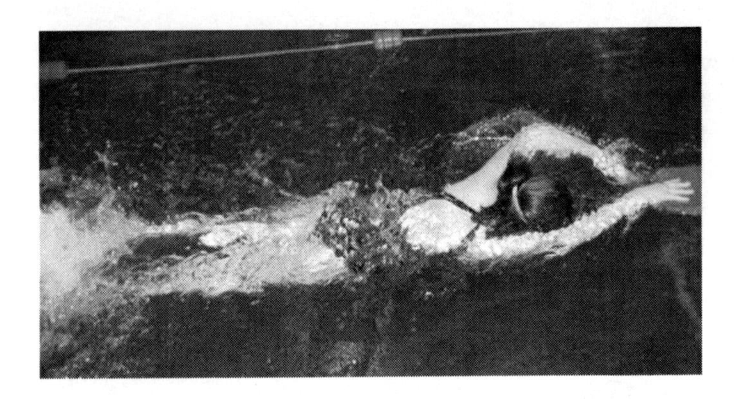

Aim: to develop coordination and correct arm pull technique.

The swimmer uses an alternating arm action. This also introduces a timing aspect as the leg kick has to be continuous at the same time.

Technical Focus

- Clean entry with fingertips first and thumb side down
- Fingers should be together
- Each arm pulls through to the hips
- Elbow leads out first
- Fingers clear the water on recovery

Key Actions

- Finger tips in first
- Brush your hand past your thigh
- Pull fast under the water
- Elbow out first
- Reach over the water surface

Elbow leads high and the hand follows over the water surface

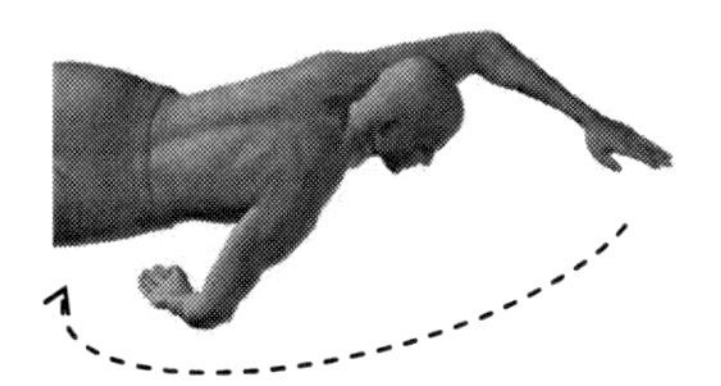

Arm pulls through towards the hip

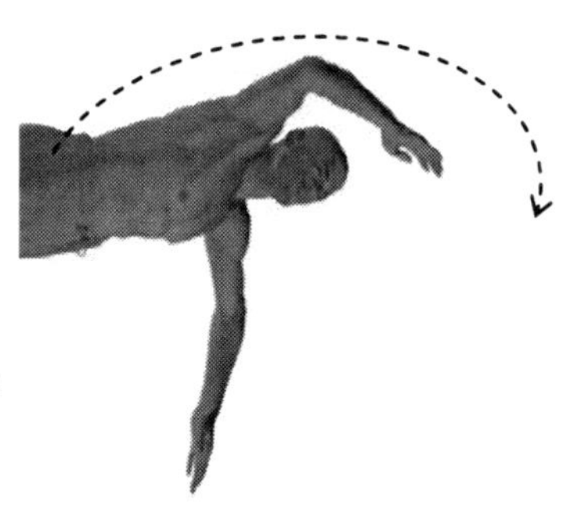

Common Faults

- Fingers are too wide apart
- Pull is short and not to the thigh
- Lack of power in the pull
- Arms are too straight on recovery
- Hand entry is wide of shoulder line

Arms: Arm action using a pull-buoy

Aim: to develop arm pull strength, technique and coordination.

This is a more advanced exercise which requires stamina and a degree of breathing technique.

Technical Focus

- Fingertips enter first with thumb side down
- Fingers should be together
- Pull should be an elongated 'S' shape
- Pull through to the hips
- Elbow comes out first
- Fingers clear the water on recovery

Key Actions
- o Long strokes
- o Smooth continuous action
- o Brush your hand past your thigh
- o Make an 'S' shape under the water
- o Elbow out first
- o Reach over the water surface

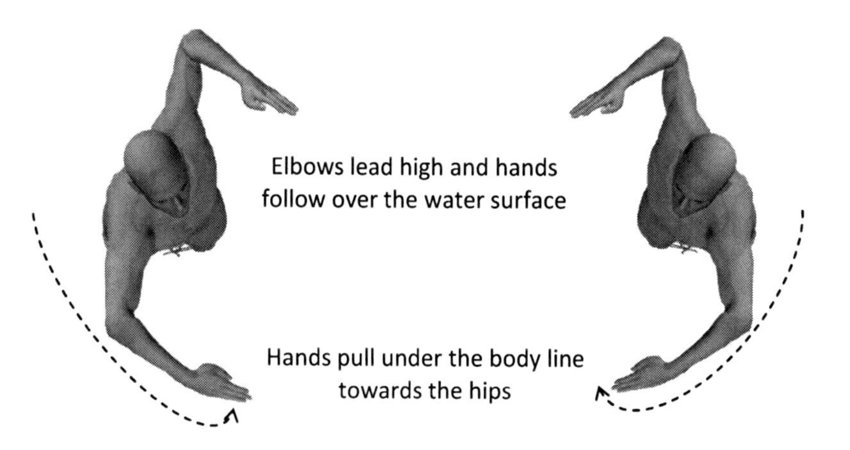
Elbows lead high and hands
follow over the water surface
Hands pull under the body line
towards the hips

Common Faults
- o Pull is short and not to the thigh
- o Lack of power in the pull
- o Arms pull too deep under water
- o Arms are too straight on recovery
- o Hand entry is across the centre line

Arms: Push and glide adding arm cycles

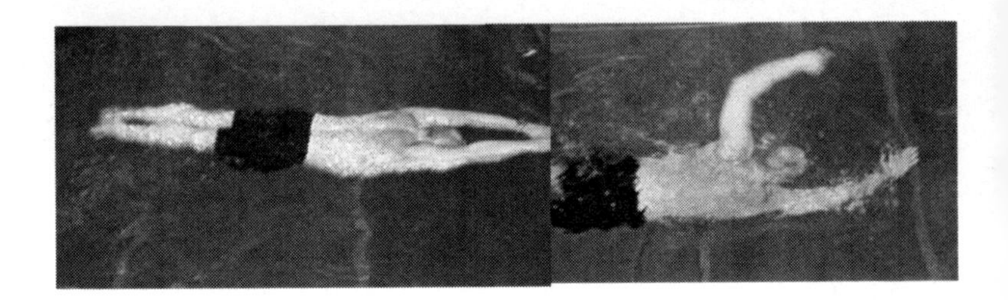

Aim: to combine correct arm action with a streamlined body position.

The swimmer performs a push and glide to establish body position and then adds arm cycles, whilst maintaining body position.

Technical Focus

- Clean entry with fingertips first
- Pull should be an elongated 'S' shape
- Pull through to the hips
- Elbow comes out first
- Fingers clear the water on recovery

Key Actions

- Finger tips in the water first
- Brush your hand past your thigh
- Make an ‘S’ shape under the water
- Elbow out first
- Reach over the water surface

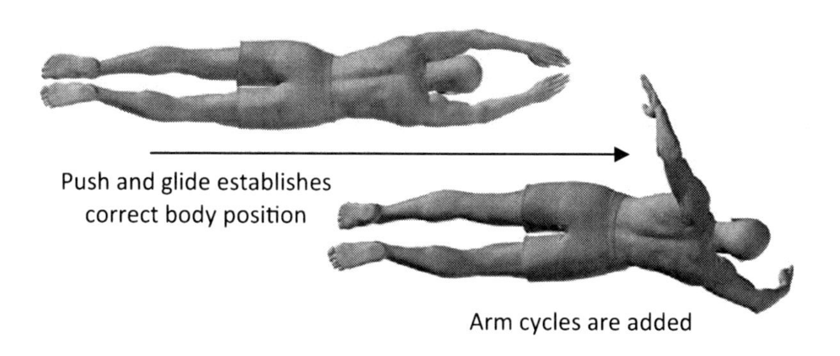
Push and glide establishes
correct body position
Arm cycles are added

Common Faults

- Pull is short and not to the thigh
- Lack of power in the pull
- Arms are too straight under water
- Arms are too straight on recovery
- Hand entry is across centre line

Breathing: Standing and holding the poolside

Aim: to practice and develop breathing technique.

The swimmer stands and holds the pool rail with one arm extended, breathing to one side. This introduces the beginner to breathing whilst having their face submerged.

Technical Focus

- Breathing should be from the mouth
- Breathing in should be when the head is turned to the side
- Breathing out should be when the face is down

Key Actions

- Breathe out through your mouth
- Blow out slowly and gently
- Turn your head to the side when you breathe in
- See how long you can make the breath last

Head turns to the side and mouth clears the water surface

Head faces forward and down

Common Faults

- Breathing through the nose
- Holding the breath

Breathing: Holding a float in front with diagonal grip

Aim: to encourage correct breathing technique whilst kicking.

The float is held in front, one arm extended fully, the other holding the near corner with elbow low. This creates a gap for the head and mouth to be turned in at the point of breathing.

Technical Focus

- Breathing should be from the mouth
- Breathing in should be when the head is turned to the side
- Breathing out should be slow and controlled

Key Actions

- o Turn head towards the bent arm to breathe
- o Breathe out through your mouth
- o Blow out slowly and gently
- o Return head to the centre soon after breathing

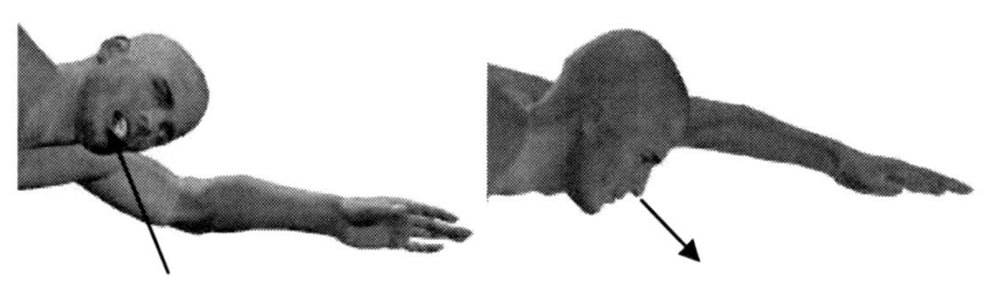

Breathe IN as the head turns out of the water

Breathe OUT as the head faces forward and down

Common Faults

- o Breathing through the nose
- o Holding the breath
- o Lifting the head and looking forward when breathing
- o Turning towards the straight arm

Breathing: Float held in one hand, arm action with breathing

Aim: to develop correct breathing technique whilst pulling with one arm.

This allows the swimmer to add the arm action to the breathing technique and perfect the timing of the two movements. The float provides support and keeps the exercise as a simple single arm practice.

Technical Focus

- Head moves enough for mouth to clear the water
- Breathing in occurs when the head is turned to the side
- Breathing out should be slow
- Breathing should be from the mouth

Float held in one hand, arm action with breathing

Key Actions

- Turn head to the side of the pulling arm
- Breathe out through your mouth
- Blow out slowly and gently
- Return head to the centre soon after breathing

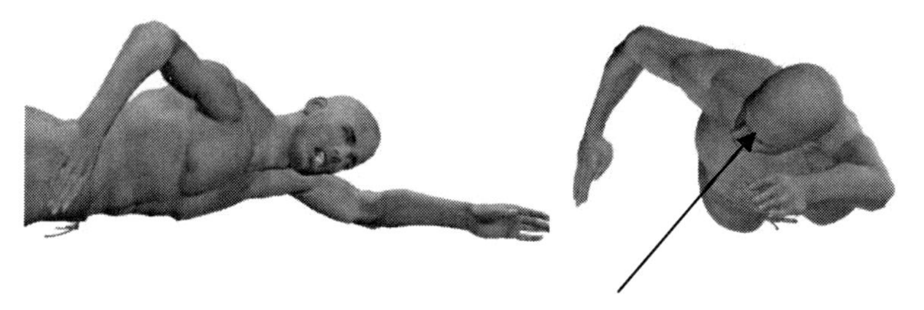

Breath IN as the arm pulls through and the head turns to the side

Common Faults

- Turning towards the straight arm
- Turning the head too much
- Breathing through the nose
- Holding the breath
- Lifting the head and looking forward when breathing

Breathing: Holding a float, alternate arm pull with breathing

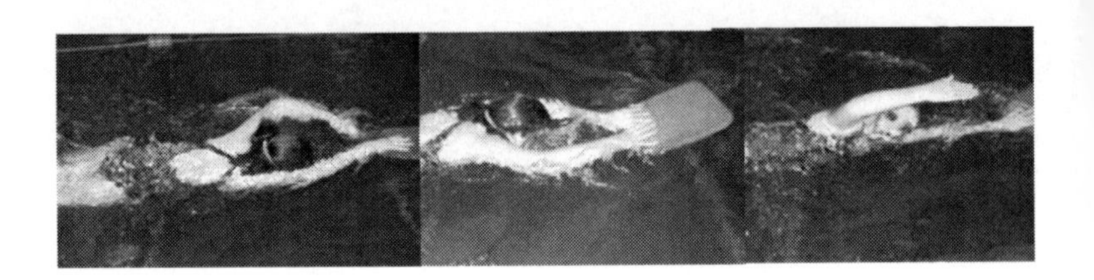

Aim: to practise bi-lateral breathing with the support of a float held out in front.

A single float is held in both hands and one arm pull is performed at a time with the head turning to breathe with each arm pull. Different arm action and breathing cycles can be used, for example; breathe every other arm pull or every three arm pulls.

Technical Focus

- Head should be still when not taking a breath
- Head movement should be minimal enough for mouth to clear the water
- Breathing in should be when the head is turned to the side
- Breathing should be from the mouth

Holding a float, alternate arm pull with breathing

Key Actions

- Keep head still until you need to breathe
- Breathe every 3 strokes (or another pattern you may choose)
- Turn head to the side as your arm pulls back
- Return head to the centre soon after breathing
- Breathe out through your mouth

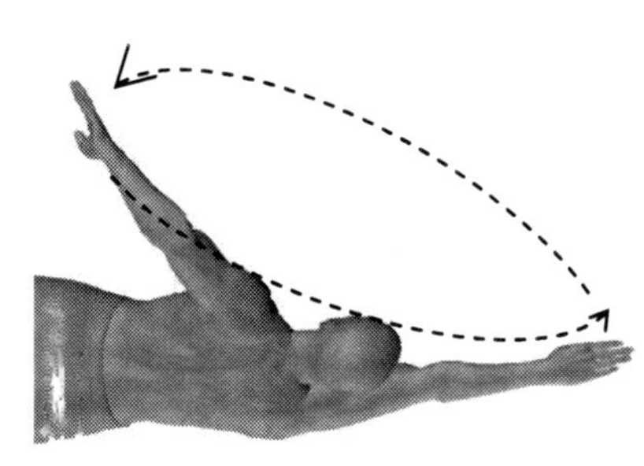

Head turns to the left side as the left arm pulls through and begins to recover

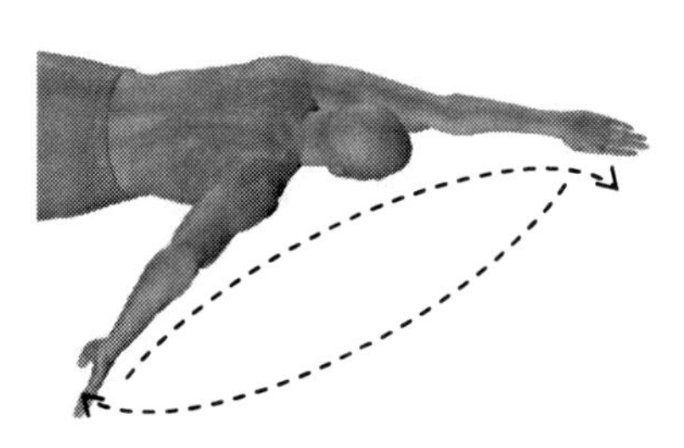

Head turns to the right side as the right arm pulls through and begins to recover

Common Faults

- Turning towards the straight arm
- Turning the head too much
- Turning the head too early or late to breath
- Lifting the head and looking forward when breathing

Timing: Front crawl catch up

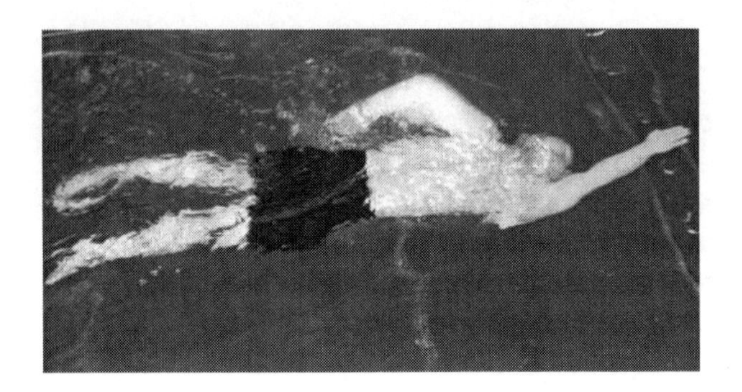

Aim: to practice correct stroke timing and develop coordination.

The opposite arm remains stationary until the arm performing the pull recovers to its starting position. This is an advanced exercise and encourages the swimmer to maintain body position and leg kick whilst practicing arm cycles.

Technical Focus

- Clean entry with fingertips first
- Pull should be an elongated 'S' shape
- Pull through to the hips
- Elbow comes out first
- Fingers clear the water on recovery

Key Actions

- Finger tips in the water first
- Brush your hand past your thigh
- Make an 'S' shape under the water
- Elbow out first
- Reach over the water surface

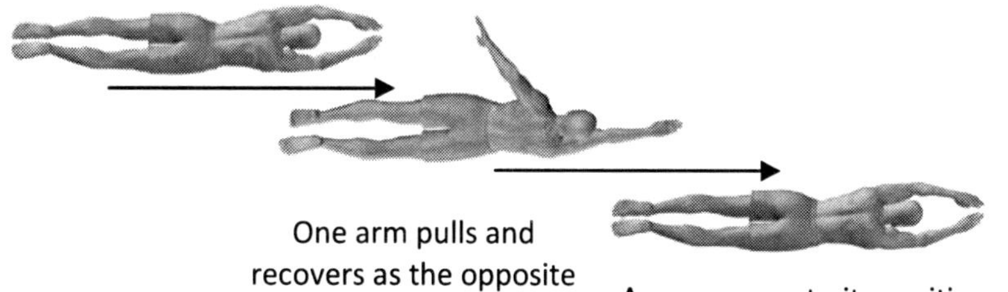

Legs kick and hands are held together
One arm pulls and recovers as the opposite arm remains in front
Arm recovers to its position in front before the opposite arm pulls and recovers

Common Faults

- One leg kick per arm pull ('one beat cycle')
- Continuous leg kick but not enough arm pulls
- Arm pull is too irregular

FRONT CRAWL: Full stroke

Aim: full stroke Front Crawl demonstrating correct leg action, arm action, breathing and timing.

Technical Focus

- Stroke is smooth and continuous
- Head in line with the body
- Legs in line with the body
- Head remains still
- Leg kick is continuous and alternating
- Arm action is continuous and alternating
- Breathing is regular and to the side
- Stroke ideally has a 6 beat cycle

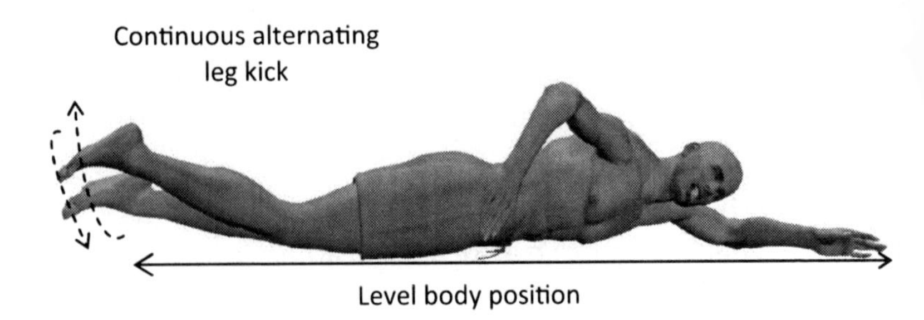

Key Actions

- Keep your head still until you breathe
- Kick continuously from your hips
- Stretch forward with each arm action
- Pull continuously under your body
- Count 3 leg kicks with each arm pull

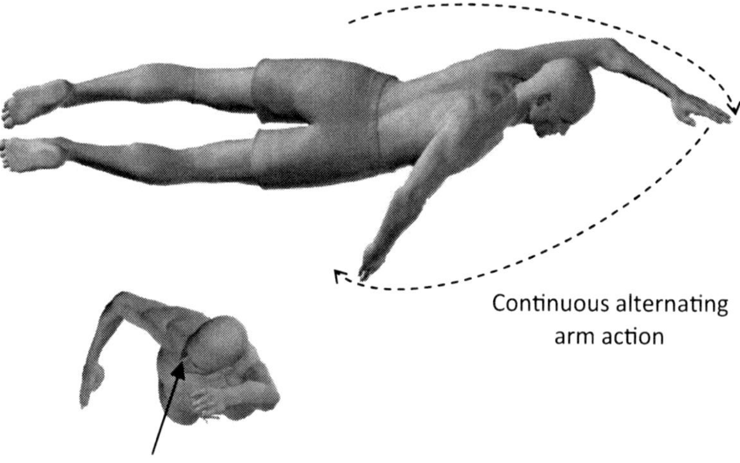

Common Faults

- Head moves from side to side
- Legs kick from the knee
- Leg action is too slow
- Arm action is untidy and splashing
- Excessive head movement when breathing
- Head is lifted, causing legs to sink
- Stroke is erratic and rushed

Front Crawl: exercise quick reference guide

Body Position

- Holding the poolside
- Static holding floats
- Moving holding floats
- Moving towards the poolside
- Push and glide

Timing

- Front crawl catch up
- Full stroke

Legs

- Sitting on the poolside
- Holding the poolside
- Holding 2 floats in front
- 1 float held out in front
- Push and glide adding kick
- Hold a float vertically

Breathing

- Standing holding the poolside
- Holding a float in one hand
- Diagonal hold on one float
- Alternating arm pull holding a float

Arms

- Standing on the poolside
- Float held in one hand
- Alternating arms holding a float
- Arms only using a pull-buoy
- Push and glide adding arm cycle

Index of stroke exercises

The Complete Guide to Swimming Front Crawl
is available in FULL COLOUR as an eBook download

Download it online now from SWIM TEACH
www.swim-teach.com

Also available from all major eBook retailers

For more information about learning to swim and improving your swimming strokes and swimming technique visit:

swim-teach.com
www.swim-teach.com

Download Complete Guides to
All Four Basic Swimming Strokes

Lightning Source UK Ltd.
Milton Keynes UK
UKOW020442041111

181435UK00002B/2/P